The 46th Gutenberg

By FRANK P. LESLIE

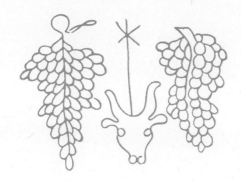

THE VAGABOND PRESS • 1960
MENOMONIE, WISCONSIN

FOREWORD

WHAT would we do if there was nothing to read? no books, magazines or papers? To whom are we indebted for the heritage of the printed page that we take for granted? We can trace our alphabet directly back to the Romans, also our letter form, for the Romans drew the most beautiful letters ever made by human hand. There are four basic letter forms: Gothic or black letter, Roman, Italic, Script. The present wide preference for the Roman letter is a survival of utility as well as beauty. The eye travels smoothly across the round graceful Roman letter and bumps over the vertical peaks of the Gothic letter. In other words, the highly legible Roman letter, redrawn first by the incunabula (the cradle of printing 1450-1500) printers and later by such immortals as Granjon, Baskerville, Caslon, Bodoni, Rogers and Goudy, has given us the surpassing beauty of the present day book.

About the middle of the 15th Century, a German genius named Johann Gutenberg perfected movable metal types and topped this great feat by printing a Bible of 643 leaves which is still the masterpiece of all printed books. Movable type meant books for the many instead of the few. In Venice, then the commercial capital of the world, Aldus Manutius, one of the great printers of all time, and himself a Greek and Latin scholar, collaborated with Erasmus, the greatest humanist of the Renaissance, and other scholars in editions of the classics for the many. From the birth of printing sprang the revival of Classicism and and the Renaissance.

Vellum was too expensive for the many copies of the books that printing made possible. Hand made paper, by some fortunate chance, was a new material ready for lower cost printing.

Today the millions around the world, eager to learn, find readily available almost limitless quantities of books and printing, thanks to the genius of our age for machine creation at costs within the reach of all.

Such a towering achievement as the Gutenberg Bible has inevitably become the first treasure of the great libraries of the world. Forty-five copies were known to exist when the following story began. The story concerns the miraculous discovery of a forty-sixth copy. You will enjoy it more when I add that no one knows how many copies were originally printed nor the date of their completion, but Henricus Cremer, rubricator (decorator) and binder, gave us our only clue and innocently made some fame for himself by inscribing notes at the end of both volumes, and I translate freely, "Thank God this is finished, 1455"

It is not easy to obtain complete accuracy in the recording of any story. I am indebted to Stanley Pargellis of the Newberry Library of Chicago, George Goodspeed, highly respected Boston dealer, Alex Wainwright of Princeton, William Jackson of Harvard, Alex Davidson, Jr. of the Grolier Club of New

York, Dorothy Miner of the Walters Gallery, of Baltimore, Messrs. Cain and Guignard of Bibliotheque Nationale, Paris, Messrs. Dring and Howard of Bernard Quaritch, London, and perhaps most of all to David Randall for material and counsel, but still more, for hours of happy companionship.

As Mrs. Leslie, my good companion in all things, once said, "Books attract the nicest people!"

THE 46th GUTENBERG

THE 46th GUTENBERG

W AY back toward the end of the 18th Century, an Englishman named Sir George Shuckburgh managed to acquire, which is an expensive word for "buy," a magnificent copy of the world's most famous book, the Gutenberg Bible. He was the last of the male line and for more than a century thereafter his female descendants handed down the book from one to the other without letting anyone know they possessed it; except, of course, the British government because a registered national treasure is not subject to the inheritance tax until sold. With every other Gutenberg copy - 45 in all - enshrined in a great public or private library, and every book dealer in the world hungry to find one more Gutenberg to sell at a fabulous price, it seems incredible, but it was true.

I am tempted to cite this case history as an all time record of women keeping a secret, but anyone who knows the English will believe that they just didn't think to tell anyone about it.

The Fiere copy, sometimes known as the Gosford-Amherst copy, was sold at Sotheby's Auction Sale in 1947 for 22,000 pounds sterling to Magg's, London book dealer who did not reveal his client. It was not generally known at the time that Mrs. Doheny of Pasadena, California, widow of Edward L. Doheny the oil man, was an unsuccessful bidder, but to the few book dealers who knew, it meant a sure customer if a copy should turn up.

David Randall, presiding over the Rare Book Department of Scribner's, called on Mrs. Doheny when in California, and assured her that he would keep his eyes open for a copy. He alerted his colleague, John Carter, the European representative of Scribner's, who also very discreetly prowled around the book world sniffing for a copy.

The first live scent developed in New York when the Trustees of the General Theological Seminary decided to sell their great copy in order to provide higher salaries for the faculty. I am indebted to Professor William Jackson of the Houghton Library at Harvard for this priceless story. The faculty, fully conscious of the desire of the Trustees to improve their incomes, voted down the proposal in a display of devotion to academic ideals that lifted the spirits of all who knew of it. Mr. Jackson dryly wondered how safe it would be to submit such a proposal to other faculties.

Our next clue came when Mr. Charles Stonehill, New Haven book dealer, met Ted Dring of Bernard

Quaritch, noted London book dealer, on the stairway in Sotheby's and imparted the important book news that John Carter had been unable to obtain the General Theological copy for Mrs. Doheny. Ted Dring walked back to his office, dreaming as would any book dealer, of the fabulous sale he might be able to make to Mrs. Doheny if he could find one more Gutenberg. He told the story to his colleague, Oliver Howard, and together they set forth on the exciting adventure.

The Reverend Dibdin, writing in "The Library Companion" 1824, in a footnote on page 13, volume II, had suggested the possible existence of such a copy somewhere in England, but that was a long time ago and nothing further had ever been heard about it.

Neither of these able men has been willing to divulge the source of the more immediate clue that sent Ted Dring to Dorset. There he found the copy he was looking for, in the possession of Lady Christian Martin, the living member of the George Shuckburgh family. The confiscatory income taxes prevailing in England had finally caught up with her and Dring was able to negotiate the purchase in collaboration with Scribner's, who acted through John Carter and David Randall in New York.

Carter then triumphantly flew the magnificent copy (only five missing leaves) to New York. Randall, no doubt trembling with excitement, called Mrs. Doheny one fine morning early in 1951, never doubting that she would be overjoyed. She wasn't. Dave told me all about it when I dropped in to visit him. He was very low in spirits. The great Shuckburgh Gutenberg was in the vault of the Fifth Avenue Bank across the street without a buyer. As Dave explained it to me, Mrs. Doheny had responded to his telephone call by saying, "But I don't want it." "Why not?" said Dave. "Because it's 1951." said Mrs. Doheny. "But what difference does that make?" "All the difference in the world," said Mrs. Doheny, "Last year was Holy Year and I had thought of buying a copy for the Holy Father, but now it is 1951 and I don't want it."

What Dave did not know at the time was that in 1950 Mrs. Doheny had acquired the Fiere copy which Lucille Miller, her librarian, records delightfully in the Doheny Catalog, saying that Mrs. Doheny had been an unsuccessful bidder for the Fiere copy in 1947 but that in 1950 a London book dealer had phoned her asking if she would like to buy it. They got together and the copy went into her library. However, it was not until the Catalog was printed several years later that this purchase and its history was publicly known. That Mrs. Doheny had wanted a second copy for the Pope in Holy Year was entirely possible.

Two years went by. One day I stopped to see Phil Duschnes, Madison Avenue book dealer, hoping to add to my own collection. He asked me if I would like to buy a Gutenberg leaf. I asked him how many he had and he replied somewhat excitedly, "Seventeen". A horrible thought struck me. I said, "Phil, did Dave Randall split up the Shuckburgh Gutenberg when he couldn't find a buyer?" I asked this question because I had known of several individuals and groups who had seriously contemplated raising the $180,000 that Scribner's was asking, but there had been no public announcement of a sale. Phil would not give out any information, referring me to Randall.

When I went to see Randall he willingly told me what had happened. Arthur A. Houghton, Jr. owned a fragmentary copy of the Gutenberg which he traded to Scribner's for the Shuckburgh and an undisclosed amount of cash. Mr. Randall had then dismantled the Houghton copy, selling the four books of the New Testament to George F. Poole, a Chicago collector. Some few years later the Eli Lilly Library of Indiana University, over which Dave Randall now presides, acquired it.

And so the great Gutenberg Bible that Sir George Shuckburgh had acquired, perhaps in 1780, when he made the Grand Tour of the Continent and which the female line had treasured for over 150 years, came to grace the library of Arthur A. Houghton, Jr. in his Queenstown home on the Eastern shore of Maryland.

As I write this story there are rumors of a fragmentary Gutenberg discovered in Belgium but I have not been able to authenticate it. Can it be that other book detectives of the Carter, Dring and Howard caliber are at work again? Who said book collecting is dull?

LOCATION OF KNOWN COPIES
AND THEIR PROVENANCE

LOCATION OF KNOWN COPIES

AUSTRIA

Perfect Copy on Paper

(1) Vienna National Bibliothek

40-41-42 line issue. With the "tabula rubricarum" (index of rubrics) printed on 4 leaves at the end. These additional leaves occur in only one other copy. (See No. 14, Munich, Bayerische, Staatsbibliothek). 2 vols., bound in red morocco.

Formerly in the Court Library of Emperor Joseph II. Transferred to the National Library early in the 19th century.

DENMARK

Imperfect Copy on Paper

(2) Copenhagen Kongelige Bibliotek

Vol. II, only. Lacks the first leaf. Bound in 17th century calf, with the device of the Gottorp Library.

This copy belonged at one time either to the monastery at Bordesholm, or to the monastery at Cismar. Eventually it came into the possession of Christian Albrecht, Prince of Gottorp and Bishop of Lubeck, whose library was acquired by the Royal Library of Denmark in 1749.

FRANCE

Perfect Copy on Vellum

(3) Paris Bibliotheque Nationale

40-41-42 line issue. 2 Vols., formerly bound in contemporary leather over wooden boards. In 1788 or shortly afterwards, it was rebound in red morocco, with the arms of Louis XVI stamped in gilt on the covers, in 4 vols.

This copy was seen in 1762 in the Benedictine Monastery of St. James, in Mainz. In 1767 it was acquired by Maugerard for Dupre de Geneste, of Mainz, whose entire library was purchased for 500 livres for the Royal Library (now the Bibliotheque Nationale).

Perfect Copy on Paper

(4)   Paris   Bibliotheque Mazarin

40-41-42 line issue. 2 Vols., bound in the 18th century red morocco, attributed to Padeloup.

The presence of this copy in the Mazarin Library was the first recorded in 1763 by the bibliographer Francois Guillaume de Bure. The term "Mazarin Bible" was formerly applied, for want of a better one, to all copies of the 42-line Bible after the wide-spread publicity the present copy attained upon de Bure's discovery.

Imperfect Copies on Paper

(5)   Paris   Bibliotheque Nationale

149 leaves lacking. Unbound. Preserved in two red morocco slipcases.

As early as 1457 this copy belonged to the Church in Ostheim. It was eventually acquired by the Electoral Library of Mainz, but in 1789 it was ceded to Maugerard, who sold it to the Royal Library (now the Bibliotheque Nationale) in 1792. This copy contains the earliest recorded date associated with the Gutenberg Bible. At the end of both volumes are notes inscribed by the rubricator and binder, Henricus Cremer, upon completion of this work: (Vol. I . . 24 August 1456; Vol. II . . . 15 August 1456.)

(6)   Saint—Omer   Bibliotheque Communale

Vol. I, only. Lacking one leaf. 40-41-42 line issue. Bound in early 18th century calf.

Formerly belonged to the Abbey of St. Bertin. Upon seculari-zation of the Abbey it was acquired by the Saint—Omer City Library.

GERMANY

Perfect Copy on Vellum

(7)   Goettigen   Universitaetsbibliothek

42 line issue. 2 Vols., bound in 16th century white calf over wooden boards.

In the 16th Century this copy was in the possession of the ducal house in the Kahlenberg—Goettingen district. It was claimed by Duke Julius of Brunswick and kept at Wolfenbuettel Library. It was acquired by the University Library of Goettingen in about 1810, after the formation of the Kingdom of Westphalia.

(8)   Berlin   Preussische Staatsbibliothek
2 leaves lacking. 40-41-42 line issue. 2 Vols., bound in 17th century calf.

Considered an old possession of the electoral family, but its presence in Berlin cannot be traced further back than 1752.

(9)   Fulda   Landesbibliothek
Vol. II, only. Bound in contemporary dark brown leather.

Formerly belonged to a certain Valentine, probably in the 16th century. It was presented by the City of Fulda to the Prince—Abbot Konstantin von Buttlar in 1723 and later returned to the State Library.

(10)   Leipzig   Universitaetsbibliothek
1 leaf lacking. 42 line issue. 4 Vols., bound in contemporary stamped pigskin, by Johann Fogel of Erfurt.

As early as 1461 this copy belonged to the Franciscan monastery in Langensalza, Saxony. The date of its acquisition by the University Library of Leipzig is not recorded.

(11)   Leipzig   Deutsches Museum fuer Buch und Schrift
1 leaf lacking. Also with other defects, restored by Pilinski (the pen-facsimile artist.) 40-41-42 line issue. 2 Vols., rebound in wooden boards, morocco backs.

Discovered in Spain in the library of the bibliophile Miro by the Parisian bookseller Bachelin—Deflorenne who exhibited it at the Paris Exposition in 1878. It was sold in the same year at auction for 50,000 francs to Lecat, whose successor Emile Lecat offered it for sale in a catalog for 70,000 francs, but eventually sold it for 25,000 francs to Albert Cohen of Berlin, who in turn sold it, also in 1878, to Heinrich Klemm of Dresden. The Klemm library was purchased by the Saxon government in 1886.

Perfect Copies on Paper

(12)   Frankfurt-am-Main   Stadtbibliothek
40-41-42 line issue. 2 Vols., recently bound in half vellum, gilt with the eagle of Frankfurt.

Formerly belonged to the Church of the College of Saint Leonhard in Frankfurt. Upon the secularization of the institute in 1803 it passed into the possession of the City Library.

(13) Leipzig   Universitaetsbibliothek
40-41-42 line issue. 2 Vols., bound in old red morocco.
    There is no record of when this copy was acquired by the University Library.

(14) Munich   Bayerische Staatsbibliothek
40-41-42 line issue. With the "tabula rubricarum" (index of rubrics) printed on 4 leaves at the end. These additional leaves occur in only one other copy. (See No. 1, Vienna, National Bibliothek). 2 Vols., bound in 18th century calf.
    Formerly belonged to the Benedictine Monastery of Andechs, near Munich. Upon the secularization of the Institute in 1803 this copy passed into the possession of the State Library.

Imperfect Copies on Paper

(15) Aschaffenburg   Stadtbibliothek
14 leaves lacking. 40-41-42 line issue. 2 Vols., bound in contemporary wooden boards, newly recovered with sheepskin.
    Formerly belonged to Friedrich Karl Joseph von Erthal, Elector of Mainz, whose library was dispersed in 1793. It was then acquired by the palace of Aschaffenburg and is now in the Hofbibliothek.

(16) Mainz   Gutenburg-Museum
Vol. II, only. Bound in early 16th century stamped leather.
    Formerly in the library of the Count of Solms-Laubach. It was acquired by the Mainz City Library in 1925.

(17) Trier   Stadtbibliothek
Vol. I, only. Bound in early 19th century calf.
    Formerly belonged to a Benedictine Monastery near Trier, whose library was acquired by the Trier City Library in 1803. (This volume is the first part of item No. 46.)

GREAT BRITAIN

Perfect Copy on Vellum

(18) London   British Museum
42 line issue. 2 Vols., rebound about 1769 in red morocco. Originally bound in 3 Vols.

This copy had formerly belonged to the Carthusian Monastery at Mainz. In 1768 it was acquired by Louis Jean Gaignat, and at the sale of his library in 1769 it was bought for 2,100 francs and 1 sou by Girardot de Prefond. About 1775 it was acquired by Count MacCarthy; at the sale of his library in Paris, 1817, it was bought for 2,600 francs by Thomas Grenville who bequeathed it to the British Museum in 1846.

Imperfect Copy on Vellum

(19)   London   Archiepiscopal Library, Lambeth Palace
New Testament, only. 190 leaves. Bound in brown morocco, about 1885.
     Formerly in the library of Archbishop Bancroft, from whom it was acquired in 1610 by the Archiepiscopal Library.

Perfect Copies on Paper

(20)   Cambridge   Cambridge University Library
40-41-42 line lissue. 2 Vols., bound in 17th or 18th century calf.
     Formerly in the possession of Lord Hopethoun, at the sale of whose library in 1889 it was purchased for £2,000 by Bernard Quaritch of London, who sold it to A. W. Young of London. It was given to Cambridge University Library in 1934.

(21)   Edinburgh   National Library of Scotland
40-41-42 line issue. 2 Vols., bound in russia leather, gilt tooled. Modern Scotch binding.
     Presented to the Advocates Library (now the National Library of Scotland), by Daniel Stewart, Lord Provost of Edinburgh, in 1781.

(22)   Eton   Eton College Library
40-41-42 line issue. 2 Vols., bound in contemporary pigskin over wooden boards, blind-stamped, by Johann Fogel of Erfurt. This is the only copy in a binding by Fogel which bears his name stamped in blind on the covers.
     Presented to Eton College in 1841 by John Fuller of Rosehill, Sussex.

13

(23) London   British Museum

42 line issue (but with some leaves of first issue). 2 Vols., bound in blue morocco for King George III.

Formerly in the Library of King George III. Transferred to the British Museum in 1829.

(24) Manchester   John Rylands Library

40-41-42 line issue. 2 Vols., bound in blue morocco, gilt tooled, with the arms of Lord Spencer stamped in blind. Binding attributed to Roger Payne.

This copy was purchased by Lord Spencer in 1814 for £80. The Spencer Library was acquired by the John Rylands Library in 1892.

(25) Oxford   Bodleian Library

40-41-42 line issue. 2 Vols., bound in blue morocco, gilt tooled by Derome le Jeune, with his label dated 1785.

According to an inscription on the former binding, described by Francois Xavier Laire, this copy was presented by Erhardus Neninger to the Carmelite friars of Heilbronn. Not later than 1785 it passed into the possession of Cardinal Lomenie de Brienne, at the sale of whose library in 1793, it was purchased by the Bodleian Library for £100.

ITALY

Imperfect Copy on Vellum

(26) Rome   Biblioteca Apostolica Vaticana

6 leaves lacking. 42 line issue. 2 Vols., bound in modern leather, blind tooled.

In 1837 this copy came into the possession of the Barberini Library, which was acquired by the Vatican Library in 1901.

Imperfect Copy on Paper

(27) Rome   Biblioteca Apostolica Vaticana

Vol. I, only. Lacking 9 leaves. Bound, about 1850, in russia leather.

Acquired by the Vatican Library in 1921 as part of the library of Cavaliere Giovanni Francesco De Rossi, from Linz, near Vienna.

POLAND

Imperfect Copy on Paper

(28)   Pelplin   Bischoefliches Priester seminar
1 leaf lacking. 40-41-42 line issue. 2 Vols., bound in contemporary
stamped leather over wooden boards, by Heinrich Coster.

Formerly in the Benedictine Monastery of Loebau, in West
Prussia, whose library was transferred to Pelplin in 1833.

PORTUGAL

Perfect Copy on Paper

(29)   Lisbon   Biblioteca Nacional
42 line issue. 2 Vols., bound in 1860 in red morocco with the royal
arms of Portugal, gilt gauffered edges. Formerly bound in green
morocco by Derome.

This copy had belonged to Cardinal Lomenie de Brienne, and at
the sale of his library in 1792 it realized 2,499 francs and 19 sous.
It was later acquired by the booksellers Borel & Co., of Lisbon, who
sold it to the Royal Library (now the Biblioteca Nacional) in 1805
for 700 milreis.

SPAIN

Perfect Copy on Paper

(30)   Burgos   Biblioteca Provincial
40-41-42 line issue. 2 Vols., bound in 16th century stamped leather
over wooden boards.

Formerly in a monastery, this copy was acquired by the Biblioteca
Provincial in 1870 when the monastery libraries were abolished by
the state.

Imperfect Copy on Paper

(31)   Seville   Biblioteca Universitaria y Provincial
New Testament, only. 190 leaves. Bound in 19th century leather.

Formerly belonged to the Jesuit College in Seville, this copy
was acquired by the Biblioteca Universitaria y Provincial upon its
foundation in 1845.

15

SWITZERLAND

Imperfect Copy on Paper

(32)   Switzerland   Private Library of Martin Bodmer
1 leaf lacking. 42 line issue. 2 Vols., in 19th century leather binding.

Formerly belonged to the monastery in Rottenbuch, but upon the secularization of the institute in 1803 this copy was acquired by the Royal Court and State Library in Munich. Considered a duplicate, it was sold at auction by Butsch, of Augsburg, in 1858, for 2,363 gulden to the Imperial Library of St. Petersburg, Russia. In 1931, by order of the Soviet Government, it was sold in London to Maggs Brothers, from whom it was acquired by the present owner.

UNITED STATES

Perfect Copy on Vellum

(33)   Washington, D. C.   Library of Congress
40-41-42 line issue. 3 Vols., bound in white calf, stamped in blind, dated 1560.

Formerly owned by the Benedictine monks of St. Blasius, in the Black Forest. In 1809 the monks took refuge in the Abbey of St. Paul, in the valley of Lavant, Carinthia, and this copy remained in the abbey until 1926, when it was bought by Dr. Otto F. H. Vollbehr, of Berlin for approximately $305,000. It was acquired by the Library of Congress in 1930 as a part of the Vollbehr collection, comprising about 3,000 specimens of 15th century printing, purchased by the United States Government for $1,500,000.

Imperfect Copies on Vellum

(34)   San Marino, Calif.   Henry E. Huntington Library
2 leaves lacking. 40-41-42 line issue. 2 Vols., bound in contemporary pigskin over wooden boards.

In 1774 this copy belonged to Otto H. von Nostitz, and about 1784 to the University of Mainz. It was offered for sale in 1801 for 1,000 francs by Merlin de Thionville, and he disposed of it to the Agent Alexander Horn of Ratisbon in about 1805. Shortly before 1817 it was acquired by the booksellers George & William Nicol in London, at whose sale in 1825 it was purchased by Henry Perkins for £504. At the Perkins sale in 1873 it was acquired by Lord Ashburnham for £3,400. At the Ashburnham sale in 1897 it was bought by Bernard Quaritch for £4,000 and sold shortly afterwards to Robert Hoe for £5,000. At the Hoe sale in 1911 it was bought by George D. Smith for Henry E. Huntington for $50,000 the highest price ever paid for a book up to that time.

(35)   New York, N. Y.   Pierpont Morgan Library
4 leaves lacking. 42 line issue. 2 Vols., bound in old brown morocco.
   Considered to be the copy which was sold by Edwin Tross in 1864 to an English collector for 15,000 francs. In 1897 it was sold by Henry Sotheran of London to J. P. Morgan.

Perfect Copies on Paper

(36)   New Haven, Conn.   Yale University Library
40-41-42 line issue. 2 Vols., bound in early 18th century calf, gilt tooled backs.
   This copy had been for centuries in the library of the Benedictine Monastery of Melk, Austria. After World War I it was sold by the monks for £11,500 to Edward Goldston, bookseller of London, who consigned it to the Anderson Galleries, New York, for sale at auction. It was bought, 15 February 1926 by Dr. A. S. W. Rosenbach for $106,000 and he sold it to Mrs. Edward S. Harkness who presented it to Yale University Library in memory of Mrs. Stephen V. Harkness.

(37)   Cambridge, Mass.   Harvard University Library
40-41-42 line issue. 2 Vols., formerly bound in blue morocco by Thouvenin. Rebound for Robert Hoe in red morocco by Mercier.
   Bequeathed in 1471 by Johann Vlyegher, a priest of Utrecht, to the Monastery at Soest near Amersfoort, Holland. In Napoleonic times it was acquired by Pierre Henri Larcher, at whose sale in Paris in 1814 it was purchased for 2,120 francs by Payne & Foss for John Lloyd. About 1840 it was acquired by Lord Ashburnham, whose son sold it to Bernard Quaritch for £3,000 in 1896. A short time later it was bought by Robert Hoe for £4,000, and in the Hoe sale in 1912 it was bought again by Quaritch for $27,500 and for him sold by Dr. A. S. W. Rosenbach to the late P. A. B. Widener. On 8 May 1944 it was presented to Harvard College Library by Mr. George D. Widener on behalf of his sister Mrs. Widener Dixon and himself.

17

(38)   New York, N. Y.   Pierpont Morgan Library
42 line issue. 2 Vols., bound in blue morocco.

In 1814 this copy belonged to Sir Mark Masterman Sykes. At the sale of his library in 1824 it was purchased for Henry Perkins by Rivington & Cochran for £199-10-0. At the sale of the Perkins library in 1873 it was bought by Bernard Quaritch for £2,690, and he sold it in the following year to Henry Huth for £3,150. At the sale of the Huth collection in 1911 it was bought by Quaritch for the Morgan collection for £5,800.

(39)   New York, N. Y.   Private Library of the Late
                                             Carl H. Pforzheimer
40-41-42 line issue. 2 Vols., bound in contemporary stamped leather over wooden boards.

Formerly belonged to James Perry, at the sale of whose library in 1822 it was purchased for 160 guineas by Thomas Joseph Pettigrew for the Duke of Sussex. At the sale of the Sussex Collection in 1844 it was bought by Bishop Robert Daly for £190. At the sale of the Daly library in 1858 it was bought by Bernard Quaritch for £596 and resold to the Earl of Crawford. In 1887 it was bought by Quaritch at the Crawford sale for £2,650 for the Earl of Carysfort, in whose library it remained until 1923. On July 2d, 1923, it was bought by Dr. A. S. W. Rosenbach for £9,500 at Sotheby's in a sale of 19 selected books from the Carysfort Library, and later sold by Dr. Rosenbach to its present owner.

Imperfect Copies on Paper

(40)   New York, N. Y.   General Theological Seminary
1 leaf lacking. 40-41-42 line issue. 2 Vols., bound in 19th century blue morocco, gilt tooled.

Formerly owned by Sir John Thorold, who acquired it about 1830. At the sale of his library in 1884 it was bought by Bernard Quaritch for £3,900. It was sold to the Rev. William Mackellar of Edinburgh, and at the sale of his library in 1898 it was again bought by Quaritch, this time for £2,950, and from him it passed to the General Theological Seminary. This copy had always been listed as perfect. However, Leaf one hundred eleven in Vol. II was a pen-and-ink facsimile, which was recently replaced with an original sheet from a dismantled copy. (See Item 4.)

(41)   Titusville, Penna.   John H. Scheide Library

5 leaves lacking. 42 line issue (but with 1 Samuel of the 40 line issue). 2 Vols., in contemporary blind stamped leather over wooden boards, probably by Fogel of Erfurt.

The second copy to come to the United States. Formerly belonged to the parish church in Erfurt, Germany. In 1870 it was offered for sale in a catalog by Albert Cohen of Berlin for 4,000 thalers and was bought in the same year by Henry Stevens of Vermont for George Brinley, of Hartford, Connecticut. At the Brinley sale, in 1881, it was bought by Hamilton Cole for $8,000, and it was later sold to Brayton Ives for $16,000. At the Ives sale in 1891 it was bought for $14,800 by James H. Ellsworth, then of Chicago. In 1924 it was bought privately by Dr. A. S. W. Rosenbach, and by him sold to the late John H. Scheide, of Titusville, Pennsylvania. Until 1934 this copy lacked 17 leaves. 12 of these missing leaves have since been supplied. In 1934 Mr. Scheide obtained two originals of those missing, and in 1937, he obtained 10 originals. In 1959, the Scheide Library, including the Gutenberg, was moved for safekeeping to the Firestone Library of Princeton University.

(42)   Queenstown, Maryland   Private Library of
                                                     Arthur A. Houghton, Jr.

5 leaves lacking (first leaf in each Vol., and the last three leaves in Vol. II). 40-41-42 line issue. 2 Vols., bound in crimson straight-grain morocco, gilt edges, by Walther, sgd and dated 1789. The binder's signature and date are placed in the center of the inside hinge at the front of the first volume. Each volume with the armorial bookplate of Sir George Shuckburgh, Bt., a member of a distinguished English family who made the Grand Tour in the early 1780's and presumably bought the book during his travels.

The Shuckburgh copy was "lost" since 1824, in which year Thomas Frognall Dibdin cited it in a footnote in his "Library Companion," Vol. 1, p. 13. From that time it disappeared from sight until early in the year 1951. It was listed in the first comprehensive census of surviving copies, that compiled by Seymour De Ricci for the Gutenberg Gesellschaft in 1911; but it was listed (as No. 52) among the "Examplaires disparus," with nothing but a reference to Dibdin as evidence that it had ever existed. Subsequent census-makers —Schwenke 1923, Reichner 1927, Johnson 1932, and Lazare 1950— remained as much in the dark as De Ricci. On February 5th, 1951,

19

Scribner's of New York announced the re-discovery of the Shuckburgh copy, which they had acquired for stock by private treaty. It was brought to the United States from England by Mr. John Carter, London representative of Scribner's, and it is the first copy to be flown across the Atlantic.

(43)   New York, N. Y.   New York Public Library

1st leaf lacking. 42 line issue. 2 Vols., bound in old blue morocco.

The first copy to cross the Atlantic. It once belonged to the Abbe Rive and was bought for 60 francs at his sale in Marseilles in 1793. At the David sale in 1803 it was purchased for 400 francs by Firmin Didot, the printer. Later, George Hibbert acquired it, and at his sale in 1829 it was sold to Cochran for £215. In 1847 it was purchased at Sotheby's at the sale of J. Wilkes by Wiley & Putnam for James Lenox of New York at the then "mad price" of £500. Until 1923 this copy lacked 4 leaves. In that year, Mr. Gabriel Wells of New York presented the Library with the originals of leaves 2, 3, and 4, in the first setting of 40 lines.

(44)   New York, N. Y.   Pierpont Morgan Library

130 leaves lacking. 42 line issue (but with 40 lines on verso of leaf 2). 2 Vols., rebound in dark brown morocco by Matthews.

According to an inscription which was partly cut away by a former binder this copy was given in 1565 by a certain N. N. from Bischofswerda, Saxony, to Melchior Gaubish, pastor of Langen-Wolmsdorf. In the 17th century it was in the possession of Heinrich von Nostitz, whose son Karl bequeathed it in 1677 to the church of Klein-Bautzen. In 1874 it was found there and sold to an Englishman for 8,850 marks. Lord Hampton then acquired it, and at the sale of his library in 1881 it was bought for £760 by Bernard Quaritch, who sold it to Theodore Irwin of Oswego, New York. The Irwin library was purchased in 1899 by J. P. Morgan.

(45)   Pasadena, Calif.   Private Library of
                                           Mrs. Edward L. Doheny

Vol. I, only. 324 leaves, bound in contemporary calf over wooden boards.

Formerly belonged to the Earl of Gosford, whose entire library was purchased by Toovey, the London bookdealer, sometime before 1880. In 1884 the Gosford Library was sold at auction by Toovey, who purchased the Bible back for £500 and sold it shortly afterwards for £600 to Lord Amherst of Hackney. At the sale of the Amherst Library in 1908 it was purchased by Bernard Quaritch for £2,050 for C. W. Dyson Perrins. At the Perrins sale, held March 10-11, 1947, at Sotheby's, it was purchased by Mr. Ernest Maggs of Maggs Brothers, London, for £22,000. Mrs. Doheny acquired the copy in 1950.

Dismantled Copy

Vol. II, only.   With 260 leaves — should be 317. Bound in 16th century leather.

This copy was found in 1828 in a peasant's house on Olewig, near Trier, by the Librarian Wyttenbach. Until 1937 it was in the Stadtbibliothek in Trier. (This is the second part of our item No. 17) On June 21st 1937 the book appeared at an auction sale at Sotheby's in London, described in the catalog as "The property of a Gentleman." It was bought by Arthur A. Houghton, Jr., with Dr. A. S. W. Rosenbach as agent for £8,000. It was acquired by Schribner's in 1953 and dismantled. The four books of the New Testament were acquired by George F. Poole, a Chicago collector and later by the Eli Lilly Library of Indiana University. Some sheets were used to "fill-in" imperfect copies, to replace pen-and-ink facsimile sheets, and others were sold to collectors as single sheets.

Typography: Lloyd Whydotski. Type: Goudy Deepdene and Cloister Black. Paper: Warren's Olde Style, Linweave Della Robbia with Lynbrook cover cloth. Ornaments: the Gutenberg paper watermark and the Shuckburgh coat of arms.